Clara Barton

Clara Barton

FOUNDER OF THE AMERICAN RED CROSS

CHRISTIN DITCHFIELD

FRANKLIN WATTS
A Division of Scholastic Inc.
New York Toronto London Auckland Sydney
Mexico City New Delhi Hong Kong
Danbury, Connecticut

Photographs © 2004: American Red Cross Museum: 56, 74; AP/Wide World Photos: 6 (Michael Dwyer), 81; Brown Brothers: cover, 72; Clara Barton Birthplace Museum, North Oxford, MA: 9; Clara Barton National Historic Site/National Park Service, Glen Echo, MD: 8, 23, 38, 50, 65, 68, 76, 89, 94; Corbis Images: 97 (AFP), 14, 61 (Bettmann), 52 (Raymond Gehman), 98 (Profiles in History), 25 (Lee Snider); Harriet B. Stowe Center, CT via SODA: 36; Hulton | Archive/Getty Images: back cover, 41, 71; Library of Congress via SODA: 2, 33; Library of Congress: cover background, 16, 27, 44, 45, 46, 54, 84, 87, 99; North Wind Picture Archives: 29, 30, 35.

Library of Congress Cataloging-in-Publication Data

Ditchfield, Christin.

Clara Barton: founder of the American Red Cross / by Christin Ditchfield.
   p. cm. — (Great life stories)

Summary: Discusses the life and work of Clara Barton, a nurse during the Civil War and founder of the American Red Cross.

ISBN 0-531-12276-X

1. Barton, Clara, 1821–1912—Juvenile literature. 2. American Red Cross—Biography—Juvenile literature.
3. Nurses—United States—Biography—Juvenile literature. [1.Barton, Clara, 1821–1912. 2. Nurses. 3. American Red Cross. 4. Women—Biography.] I. Title. II. Series.

HV569 .B3D58 2004

361.7'634'092—dc22

2003013343

Contents

BIRTHPLACE OF
CLARA BARTON
FOUNDER OF THE
AMERICAN RED CROSS

Clara Barton was born in this house on December 25, 1821. Her family home is now a museum.

ONE

From "Tot" to Teacher

On Christmas Day in 1821, the Barton family received a very special Christmas gift—a new baby girl. Clarissa Harlowe Barton was born at home on the family's farm in North Oxford, Massachusetts. Stephen and Sarah Barton named their youngest daughter after a favorite aunt, who in turn had been named after the heroine of a popular novel. There were four other children in the family already. When Clarissa was born, Dolly was seventeen, Stephen was fifteen, David was thirteen, and Sally was almost eleven. They loved having a new little sister and treated her like a doll or a pet. They all took turns playing with her and caring for her. The older children never called Clarissa by her proper name. Instead, they nicknamed her "Tot" and "Baby," and later "Clara."

A FAMILY OF TEACHERS

Because she was so much younger than her siblings, Clara said, "I had no playmates, but in effect six fathers and mothers." Each one of her brothers and sisters helped look after Clara. Each one taught her to enjoy some of his or her own favorite activities. Dolly was passionate about learning. She loved to read and study, and she made sure that Clara did too. At the age of three, Clara could read and spell simple words. Stephen had a gift for working with numbers. He introduced Clara to "figures," or mathematics.

David was the more adventurous and athletic member of the family. He taught Clara to ride a horse by the time she was five years old. He also taught her how to run fast, tie a strong knot, and throw a ball "like a boy." Sally was the closest in age to Clara. The two girls shared a bedroom in the old farmhouse. They often stayed up late, reading their beloved storybooks or looking up faraway places in an atlas.

Clara may have learned a lot from her brothers and sisters, but her parents taught her many things, as well. Captain Barton was a hardworking and successful man, recognized as a leader in the community. He was known for his generosity and kindness to the less fortunate. The entire Barton

Clara's father, Captain Stephen Barton, was an important influence on her.

family had a long history of involvement in politics and war. Before they came to the United States, Clara's ancestors fought in England's War of the Roses. Her grandfather was a "rebel" in the Revolutionary War. Captain Barton himself had been a soldier in the Indian Wars—a long series of battles between American Indians and white settlers on the frontier.

Clara spent countless evenings curled up in front of the fireplace, listening to her father tell war stories. She begged him to tell them again and again. Together, Clara and her father drew maps of the battlegrounds and reenacted scenes from the wars. Although she didn't realize it at the time, Clara was being prepared for her own wartime experiences. One day, she would have plenty of her own adventure stories to tell.

Clara's mother was an energetic woman with a fiery temper. Sarah Barton didn't have time for nonsense. She always did "two days' work in one," and she insisted that her daughters work hard too. At an early age, Clara learned to help with cooking, sewing, and other household chores.

Sarah kept busy at home. She had little time for or interest in the outside world. Yet she held strong views on many of the important issues of her time. An abolitionist, Sarah signed a number of petitions demanding an end to the practice of slavery. She believed that women should have the

Clara's mother, Sarah, was a hard worker, taking care of her children and running the family household.

same rights and freedoms as men, and she passed these convictions along to her daughters. As Clara later recalled, "I must have been born believing in the full rights of women to all privilege and position which nature and justice accorded her. . . . When as a young woman I heard the subject discussed, it seemed ridiculous that any reasonable person should question it."

Clara was only four years old when she started attending school. Her teachers couldn't believe that the tiny girl could already spell words such as "artichoke." In Clara, they found a bright and eager pupil. Several of her teachers took a special interest in Clara, encouraging her to keep learning and growing as a person throughout her lifetime.

A PAINFUL CHILDHOOD

Although she had a family that loved her dearly, in some ways Clara did not have a very happy childhood. She once said, "In the earlier years of my life, I remember nothing but fear."

Clara was afraid of snakes, thunderstorms, and runaway horses. She was even more afraid of people. As a shy and sensitive girl, she shrank from any and all contact with strangers. She even felt uncomfortable talking to people she knew. Clara lived in constant fear of doing or saying the wrong thing. She dreaded making mistakes. Her family teased her endlessly, laughing over all the silly things "Baby" had said or done. They meant it in fun, but it embarrassed Clara and hurt her deeply.

From time to time, the older Bartons grew so busy with their own affairs that they forgot about Clara. They didn't notice that her clothes were wearing out or that her shoes were too tight. Clara was afraid to ask for new things because she didn't want to be a burden to her family. But when they neglected her needs, Clara felt unimportant.

When Clara was six years old, tragedy struck the Bartons. Clara's oldest sister, Dolly, had a nervous breakdown. In those days, people didn't understand mental illness. There were no treatments available for those who suffered from it. When Dolly became violent and hysterical, she was locked in a room with bars on the windows—to keep her from hurting herself or someone else. Not long after her breakdown, Dolly died.

THE TROUBLE WITH CLARA

By the time Clara was eight years old, her family had begun to notice her unusual fears and shyness. Her parents thought that sending her to boarding school would help her overcome her fear of strangers. It was a terrible mistake. Far from her family and surrounded by unfamiliar people and places, Clara became so distraught that she could not speak. She stopped eating, and her health declined. The school's teachers grew alarmed and decided that Clara should be sent home at once.

Back on the farm, Clara tried to forget the awful experience. She played with her dog, Button. She went for long rides on Billy, a new horse her father had given her. Stephen and David had moved into town and started a mill business together. Sally got married. But Clara was not alone in the house. One of her uncles had died, leaving a wife and four children without anyone to care for them. Captain Barton took over the uncle's farm, and for a time, the two families lived together. Clara didn't have very much in common with the girls, but she adored the boys— Otis and Jerry. They reminded her of her brothers, whom she sorely missed. The cousins chased each other through the fields, climbing trees, sword fighting, and playing ball. The boys soon found that Clara could run as fast and climb as high as they could.

Although she got along well with the boys, Clara was still shy. She cried when her feelings were hurt and hid when she was frightened or upset about something. Clara still worried about being a burden to her family. She looked for ways to be useful. Clara took over the care of all the ducks, chickens, and cats on the farm. She learned how to milk the cows. When hired hands came to repair the barns and buildings, Clara followed them around and watched them work. With her parents' permission, the workers taught Clara how to mix paints, hang wallpaper, and varnish wood.

THE ACCIDENT

Stephen and David's mill business did very well. The two brothers were building a new barn together, when David slipped and fell off the roof. He was badly hurt, and the doctors thought he would die. To everyone's astonishment, little Clara took charge of the patient at once.

"I was distressed beyond measure at his condition," Clara remembered. "From the first days and nights of illness, I remained near his side. . . . I learned to take all directions for his medicines from his physician . . . and to administer them like a genuine nurse."

David got worse before he got better. For two years, Clara nursed him back to health. She was so gentle and kind that David refused to have anyone care for him but his little sister. For the first time in her life, Clara felt needed. She knew she was doing something worthwhile that would help someone else. In her concern for David, she forgot to be afraid. Instead, she was calm and confident in her abilities as a competent nurse. The Bartons could hardly believe the change in their youngest daughter.

Eventually, David recovered from his injuries. He no longer needed the constant care of his faithful little nurse. Clara had mixed emotions about his recovery. She was delighted to see her beloved brother healthy again, but she missed feeling needed. She missed having a sense of responsibility and purpose—the satisfaction that came from helping someone else. She did not know what she would do next.

For a while, Clara cared for her nieces and nephews—Sally's children. Then she took a job weaving cloth at Stephen and David's Satinet Mill. Unfortunately, two weeks after she started work, the factory burned down. Clara kept looking for something useful to do. She

Bad Medicine

In the 1800s, doctors knew very little about the causes of common illnesses and infections. They didn't understand the importance of sterilizing equipment. There were few effective medications. Most of the popular cures did more harm than good. Patients who were given opium and strychnine often lost their hair and teeth. Some suffered nerve damage from these drugs. Doctors thought it was necessary to apply leeches (a type of small bloodsucking worm) to the skin to "suck out bad blood." This treatment left patients weak and vulnerable to all kinds of infectious diseases.

tutored poor children in their schoolwork. She nursed neighboring families who were stricken with smallpox until she became ill herself.

One day, sixteen-year-old Clara had fallen asleep on the sofa, when she was awakened by the sound of voices in the next room. Clara heard her mother talking to a stranger about her "difficult" daughter. The stranger was Dr. L. N. Fowler, an English phrenologist. Phrenologists believed that the shape of a person's skull determined his or her personality and behavior. By studying the lumps and bumps of the head, one could discover a person's skills and talents and find out what type of career he or she was best suited for.

Although it was popular in the nineteenth century, doctors and scientists now know that phrenology is not accurate. Nevertheless, Fowler did have some remarkable insight into Clara's character. He told her mother, "The sensitive nature will always remain. She will never assert herself. She will suffer wrong first, but for others she will be perfectly fearless." On her own, Clara would always be timid and shy. When she

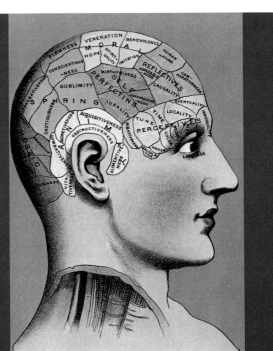

This illustration shows how phrenologists viewed the human skull. The different parts of the skull were thought to relate to different attributes, such as hope and cautiousness.

How Old Was She?

Some biographies say Clara was fifteen years old when she began teaching. Others say sixteen, seventeen, or eighteen. There is confusion about her age at other times in her life, as well, because Clara often lied about her age. As a young teacher, she wanted to appear older and more mature than her students. Later, Barton worried that people would think she was too old to handle her responsibilities. To disguise her age, she wore makeup and dyed her hair. When asked about her childhood, she subtracted a few years here and there. It has taken historians a lot of time and effort to untangle the truth.

was caring for others, she would be brave and strong. Fowler had this advice: "Throw responsibility upon her. She has all the qualities of a teacher!"

Clara could not have been more shocked at this suggestion. It terrified her to even think of standing alone in front of a room full of schoolchildren. But the Bartons were convinced that this was the perfect solution to Clara's problems. Somehow, they persuaded her to study for her teaching certificate. The next spring, at the age of seventeen, Clara passed the test. The school board immediately offered her a teaching position at a school across town. Clara was about to begin a brand-new life.

This illustration, which appeared in an educational publication in the 1800s, shows what a one-room schoolhouse looked like during this time period.

Restless Years

On the first day of school, forty pupils squeezed into the shabby one-room schoolhouse. They were anxious to meet their new teacher. The students ranged in age from toddlers to teenagers. Some were the same age as Barton. "We had all been children together," Barton recalled. The women in Barton's family had lengthened her skirts and taught her how to pile her hair high on her head, so that she would look older. They made her a pretty green dress to wear on her first day as a teacher. Barton treasured that dress and kept it for the rest of her life.

Miss Barton was only five feet tall. Many of her students towered over her. As Barton stood before the class, she suddenly realized that she had no idea how to start the day! Reaching over her desk, her hand fell on a Bible. She opened it and began reading to her students. Almost immediately, Barton's gentle and friendly manner won the hearts of her students. Her enthusiasm was contagious. She made math, science, and history fascinating. The children couldn't wait to learn more.

Four of the boys in her class had a reputation for rough and rowdy behavior. There were rumors that their wild pranks had caused the previous teacher to quit the school. At recess, some of the older boys began their rough play. They were startled when their tiny teacher decided to join their game. All the skills Barton had learned from her brother David came in handy that day. The boys were amazed by her athletic ability. She could throw a ball better than they could. "My four lads soon perceived that I was no stranger to their sports or tricks," Barton said. "When they found . . . that if they won a game it was because I permitted it, their respect knew no bounds."

A RESPECTED TEACHER

Soon school officials recognized Barton's gift for teaching and the superb control she exercised over her class. Barton never yelled at her students, threatened them, or punished them. She didn't have to. The students obeyed her because they loved her and wanted to please her. At the end of the school term, Barton was awarded the highest standing in North Oxford for discipline in the classroom. More important to her, she had earned a special place in the hearts of her students and their families.

Neighboring towns invited Barton to come and teach at their schools. Barton accepted a position in Charlton, not far from North

Oxford. Still, she would have to move away from her parents' home. As hard as it was to leave her family, her experience as a teacher had given her new self-confidence. For the next ten years, Barton moved from school to school, often taking over problem schools and setting them straight. These schools lacked organization and discipline. They held classes in broken-down old buildings, barely scraping together even the most basic supplies. The students were disobedient, disrespectful, and reluctant to learn. Other teachers had come and gone, giving up on what seemed like a hopeless situation. But Barton loved the challenge. She became widely respected and well known for her superior teaching ability. She had her pick of schools. She could choose whatever position she wanted. One school asked her to teach the longer and more difficult winter term (often taught by male teachers) at the smaller salary paid to women who taught summer school. Barton refused.

"I may sometimes be willing to teach for nothing," she said. "But if paid at all, I shall never do a man's work for less than a man's pay." The school board gave her the salary she asked for.

One of Barton's most ambitious projects was to reorganize and redistrict the school system in her own hometown. The success of the mills and factories had brought many new families to North Oxford. The city had grown rapidly, but the school system had not kept up. The school buildings were old and crumbling. Their location was no longer convenient to the neighborhoods they were meant to serve. There were no schools at all in the areas where the mill workers and their families lived. Barton worried that these children would not have the opportunity to learn. Her brother Stephen shared her concern. As a mill owner, Stephen believed that it was important to provide education for his employees' children. Unfortunately, many of the other townspeople weren't convinced. They feared that renovations would cost the town too much money. The town's wealthier people did not feel it was their responsibility to provide schools for poor children. Together, Clara and Stephen campaigned for more than a year to persuade the town council and the school board to consider the matter. One of their opponents was their own father, community leader and school-board member Captain Stephen Barton. But in the end, after a lengthy struggle, Clara and Stephen convinced the citizens of North Oxford that it was time to overhaul their educational system.

Barton was actively involved in every step of the process. In Barton's day, most schools were located in buildings that had originally been used for something else. They were not created with teachers and children in mind. These schools did not have separate classrooms for each grade level. Instead, all of the students studied in one room. Every desk was built the same size—too large for preschool children and too small for teenagers. Barton came up with the idea of building the classrooms with gently sloping floors. At the front of the room, the smaller students could sit properly at their desks and touch their feet to the ground. At the back of the class, larger students had much more room. As an expert teacher, Barton designed all of the classrooms for the new school buildings, making sure there were clocks, maps, and blackboards in the right places.

Barton decided that she herself would teach at the first school for the mill workers' children. It was a tough assignment. She had more than seventy pupils ranging in age from four to twenty-four—all in one small room! Some of her students were Americans, but many others were immigrants. Along with their families, they had come from Great Britain, Ireland, France, and other European countries. Quite a few of them had trouble speaking English. To help improve their language skills, Barton instructed her students to practice reading aloud during their class time. She encouraged them to recite poetry and act out their favorite plays and stories. Barton discovered that her new students loved to perform. Before long, crowds began gathering outside the schoolroom to listen to the students during the day. Eventually, the students held "concert readings" in the evenings. People came from all over town to enjoy the performances. The mill workers' school proved to be a great success.

Between school terms, Barton spent time with family and friends, especially her nieces and nephews. She went horseback riding and wrote poetry. She even tried her hand at flower arranging. Though she never felt completely at ease among strangers, Barton learned to make conversation and form lasting friendships with new acquaintances. Because of her reputation as a teacher, her insights and opinions were respected by others. She was not "Tot" anymore—a baby to be teased and laughed at. She was an accomplished educator.

TIME FOR A CHANGE

In 1850, Barton turned twenty-nine years old. She had been teaching school for more than ten years. Barton began to feel restless and dissatisfied with her life. She needed a new challenge. When she had first started teaching, Barton worried that she did not know enough to be a teacher. There was still so much she wanted to learn. After years of teaching experience, Barton surprised everyone by announcing that she was going back to school. She enrolled as a student at the Clinton Liberal Institute in Clinton, New York, one of the few academies that accepted female students.

Barton's Admirers

As Barton outgrew her shyness, she became a popular guest at parties and social events. Many young men found her attractive, and Barton enjoyed their attention. She often wore red, a color that complemented her deep brown eyes and dark hair. She smiled and laughed a lot. She had opinions on interesting subjects. Over the years, Barton received several marriage proposals. According to her diary, she fell in love a number of times. Yet in those days, it was hard for an intelligent and successful woman like Barton to find a husband who could appreciate her busy lifestyle. Many people believed that a woman could not combine marriage and a career. More than half of the first generation of college-educated women in the 1880s and 1890s remained unmarried, and Barton was one of them.

The other students were much younger than Barton. She didn't want to stand out or draw attention to herself in the classroom, so she kept her age a secret. She told no one—not even the professors—about her past teaching experience. Barton wanted to make the most of her time at the institute. She took as many classes as the school would allow. These college courses were difficult. Barton studied for hours and hours a day, loving every minute of it.

After a year at the Clinton Institute, Barton realized she was running out of money to pay for her classes. While she had been 200 miles away (321.8 kilometers) at the academy, her mother had died. By the time Barton found out about her mother's death, it was too late to attend the funeral. Missing her family, Barton decided to return home to North Oxford. For a few months, she rested from her studies and visited with her loved ones. But Barton could never be happy just sitting around and doing

This photograph of Barton was taken during her time in Clinton, New York. It is considered to be the earliest known photograph of Barton.

nothing. When friends told her of a teaching position in Cedarville, New Jersey, she gladly accepted it. The Cedarville students were known to be wild and undisciplined. Just as before, Barton quickly won them over. She delighted in bringing order to the classroom.

There was one thing Barton didn't like about her new job. All of the schools in New Jersey were subscription schools, which meant that students had to pay a monthly fee to the teacher in order to attend. Barton had to bill her students personally to receive her salary. She hated having to remind the children to bring in their money.

One day, Barton took a trip to Bordentown, New Jersey. There, she saw a group of boys playing in the street. When she asked them why they weren't in school, they explained that their families could not afford to send them. This broke Barton's heart. She firmly believed that education should be free. Every child should have the opportunity to learn. Barton went to see the Bordentown school board. She told them that she wanted to open a free school for poor children. If the town would help provide a building and supplies, she would teach without pay. At first, the members of the school board were uncertain. New Jersey had never had a free public school. They were afraid the townspeople would not support it. They thought poor parents might be embarrassed to send their children to a free school. The children on the street were rough and unmannered, and the school board wasn't sure that Barton could control them.

Barton was absolutely determined to make her new dream come true. She persuaded the members of the school board to give her a chance. The board agreed to clean up and repair a broken-down schoolhouse at the edge of town. They put advertisements in the newspaper and posted signs announcing the start of the new school. On the first day, only six boys showed up for class. They were more than a little nervous and not quite sure what to expect from their teacher. Barton read amazing adventure stories to them. She showed them maps of places they had never heard of and taught them interesting things about science and history. The boys were so excited that they could hardly wait to tell their families what they had learned. Early the next morning, twenty students waited for Barton at the schoolhouse door. In a matter of weeks, there were so many new students that the school board had to hire another teacher to help Barton.

The school became enormously successful. Students started leaving subscription schools to attend Barton's classes. The townspeople got very excited about her work. Everyone was talking about this wonderful free public school. In just two years, Schoolhouse Number

This is the school that Barton founded in New Jersey. It was one of the first free schools.

One had grown to enroll more than six hundred students. The community came together to build a new two-story brick school building with eight classrooms. They bought new books and supplies and hired more teachers.

But when the next term started, Barton was shocked to learn that the school board had decided to replace her as head of the school. Because the school had grown so large and prosperous, they felt that a man should be in charge of it. The new male principal would be paid twice as much as Barton was paid. She would be his assistant.

This infuriated Barton. She had built the school from nothing. It was successful because of her vision and hard work. And now it was being taken from her, simply because she was a woman. She disliked Principal J. Kirby Birnbaum from the start, disagreeing with his strict rules. She thought he was critical of her and her work. Many arguments broke out among the staff, with some teachers siding with Barton and others with the principal. The whole situation made Barton miserable. The anxiety and stress affected her health. She grew tired and weak. One day, when she got up to teach, she found she could not speak. She had completely lost her voice. Barton promptly resigned from the school.

A DIFFERENT WORLD

It was a great relief to Barton to be free from the disastrous situation at Bordentown. But she was uncertain about what she would do next. She had been teaching for fifteen years; she was thirty-two years old, with no husband or family of her own. She was weary and discouraged. Thinking that warmer weather would help her throat, Barton made a trip to the nation's capital, Washington, D.C. Her love for learning led her to tour all the historic sites. She spent hours poring over books in the Library of Congress. She sat in the galleries of the House of Representatives and the Senate and watched lawmakers at work. Barton became good friends with Alexander De Witt, a congressman from Massachusetts. Through De Witt, she met Charles Mason, the commissioner of the United States Patent Office. Mason could see that Barton was intelligent and ambitious. She understood politics and could discuss all the current issues of the day. He offered her a job as a clerk at the Patent Office.

When she accepted his offer, Barton became one of only a handful of women to hold an official job with the United States government. In addition to granting patents for new inventions,

Barton befriended Alexander De Witt, a congressman from her home state.

the office sponsored scientific research and collected historical artifacts. It was a busy and exciting place to be. Barton loved her new job. She worked in the office from 9:00 A.M. to 3:00 P.M. each day, filing legal documents and filling out paperwork. In the days before typewriters, computers, or copy machines, everything had to be written—and copied—by hand. In her clear, strong handwriting, Barton copied as many as one thousand pages per month. She received what was then a huge salary for a woman: $1,400 per year. At that time, female book-keepers earned approximately $500 per year. Dressmakers earned about $300 per year. As a teacher, Barton had only been paid $250 per year. This was an incredible opportunity for Barton.

"My situation is delightfully pleasant," Barton wrote to her family. "There is nothing in the world connected with it to trouble me and not a single disagreeable thing to do, and no one to complain of me."

In time, some of her male coworkers did try to cause problems for Barton. They didn't think women should hold important jobs or get paid as much as men. They blew cigar smoke in Barton's face and made rude comments when she walked by. Others spread rumors that questioned her moral character. Barton simply ignored them. Mason discovered that his newest employee was extremely hardworking and dependable. Over and over, she proved that she could handle all of the responsibilities given to her. She had terrific organizational skills. At Mason's request, Barton began finding new ways to make the Patent Office more effective and efficient. Together, they made many improvements in office policy. For three years, Barton faithfully served her country by working at the United States Patent Office. Yet her greatest service to the United States was still to come.

The U.S. Patent Office

The United States Patent Office grants patents, which are legal documents that give an individual or a company the exclusive right to produce and sell a particular object or invention. The office also registers copyrights and trademarks. These legal documents are designed to prevent people from stealing others' ideas. If people copy someone else's patented work without permission, they can be fined or sent to jail. Created more than two hundred years ago, the Patent Office reports to the secretary of commerce and the president of the United States on patent, trademark, and copyright protection.

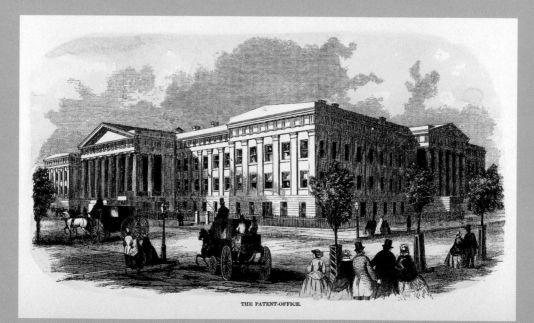

THE PATENT-OFFICE.

After working at the Patent Office, Barton had difficulty finding a new challenge to tackle when she returned home.

THREE

Angel of the Battlefield

In 1857, Clara Barton lost her job at the United States Patent Office. A new Democratic president had been elected, and he appointed his own commissioners for government offices. Charles Mason was replaced as head of the Patent Office. The new commissioner fired many employees—including Barton—and hired his own friends and acquaintances to take their jobs. Barton had no option but to return to North Oxford.

For the next three years, she stayed with various relatives and tried to make herself useful. For a time, Barton moved into the home of her older brother David and his wife Julia. Barton helped care for her four nieces and nephews. She did more than her share of household chores, including cooking, cleaning, and laundry. All the while, she looked for a new job that would be appropriate for a woman of her skill and experience. This turned out to be an impossible task. Most businesses outside Washington refused to hire women as clerks. Time and time again, Barton applied for an office position—any office position—only to be told that the company had "no room for ladies." Barton's financial resources were quickly drained, and her family treated her like a burden. People couldn't understand why she didn't get married and settle down or go back to teaching.

In Washington, Barton had held a job with an important government agency. She had been respected by prominent members of society. Barton had maintained a lively and intellectual circle of friends. She debated politics with congressmen. She attended balls, galas, and affairs of state. She had nothing in common with North Oxford's farming community. She felt very lonely.

To pass the time, Barton sewed quilts, studied French, and took drawing lessons. As always, Barton's heart was drawn to needy people. She looked for opportunities to offer comfort, compassion, and practical assistance. Barton spent a good deal of her time nursing her nephew Irving, who suffered from a chronic illness. Although she was struggling financially herself, she paid for many of his medical treatments. She also sent money to another family member to pay for that relative's education. Some of her less-fortunate relatives took advantage of her kindness. They continually demanded more money. Somehow, whatever she gave them was never enough.

A SECOND CHANCE

Barton's only hope was to return to Washington and regain her position at the Patent Office. She eagerly followed the news from the political world and kept in touch with her government friends. Finally, in 1860, the tide turned. Abraham Lincoln was elected president and the Republican Party came into power. Barton's friends were able to secure another position for her at the Patent Office. She returned to Washington in time to attend President Lincoln's inauguration. Barton couldn't have been happier.

The best way to keep a job in Washington was to have friends and supporters in high office. So Barton took care to develop and strengthen her political friendships. She requested a meeting with Senator Henry Wilson to discuss her concerns about problems in the Patent Office. Senator Wilson was a powerful and influential man. Like

The Republican Party came to power in Washington, D.C., when Abraham Lincoln was elected as the sixteenth president of the United States.

Barton, he had great organizational and leadership skills. Wilson and Barton became lifelong friends. Over the years, Senator Wilson would often come to Barton's assistance.

On the surface, it seemed that Washington had changed very little during Barton's absence. But there was talk of trouble. Sharp disagreements had arisen between the northern and southern states. One cause of disagreement was slavery. For roughly two hundred years, African people had been kidnapped from their homes, brought to the United States, and sold as slaves. In the South, farmers grew large quantities of cotton and other crops. They depended on slave labor to help them run their vast plantations. In the northern states, most people worked in factories or on small family farms. They did not have the same need for labor. Many people in the North believed that slavery was wrong. They decided to make slavery illegal in their states, and they tried to force the South to do the same.

Not everyone in the South supported slavery. But many believed in states' rights, which meant that each state had the right to make its own laws. They believed that the national government should not make decisions for them and should not make laws without each state's approval. The Southern states grew angry at the national government. They felt that the government made laws that treated them unfairly. In 1860, South Carolina, on hearing the news of Abraham Lincoln's election, announced that it would secede from the country. It would no longer be a part of the United States of America. The Northern states insisted that South Carolina did not have the right to secede. They wanted the president to send armies to South Carolina to take control of the state. South Carolina wanted the rest of the Southern states to join it in forming a new country, the Confederate States of America. The Civil War began when Confederate forces fired on the U.S. government outpost at Fort Sumter in Charleston harbor on April 12, 1865.

Clara Barton had always been taught that slavery was wrong. As a teacher herself, she often read *Uncle Tom's Cabin* aloud to her students. This popular novel by Harriet Beecher Stowe exposed the evils of slavery.

The Civil War began with the battle at Fort Sumter.

Barton, however, was not a "fiery abolitionist" like her mother. She did not pass around petitions or attend demonstrations against the practice of slavery. She thought that the idea of secession was ridiculous. Like many people in the North, she expected that the Southern states would come to their senses sooner or later and that the conflict would eventually die down. She was shocked when war broke out.

Harriet Beecher Stowe

Harriet Beecher Stowe described herself as simply "a wife and mother," but she was also one of the most prominent and successful authors of the nineteenth century. In 1851, Stowe wrote *Uncle Tom's Cabin*, a novel about the brutality of slavery. The controversial book quickly sold more than one million copies and was translated into twenty languages. For the first time, many people began to think about the injustice of slavery. They demanded an end to the evil practice. In 1862, Stowe was introduced to President Abraham Lincoln. He greeted her by saying, "So you are the little woman who wrote the book that started this great war!"

A DESPERATE NEED

At the time, there was no national army. Every state had its own militia made up of small groups of ordinary citizens who could protect or defend their neighborhoods in an emergency. President Lincoln called on state militias to come to Washington to form an army that would put an end to the rebellion in the South. The Sixth Massachusetts Regiment was one of the first to respond. These volunteer troops were young and inexperienced, but they were eager to serve. Almost forty of them had been Clara Barton's students. On their way to Washington, they changed trains in Baltimore, Maryland. The citizens of Baltimore supported the South. Without warning, they attacked the new soldiers, hurling insults at them, throwing bricks, and seizing their luggage. Before long, shots rang out. Four soldiers and twelve civilians were killed, and thirty more were wounded. People in Washington heard about the attack and ran to meet the trains as they arrived. Barton joined them.

The soldiers had no food, blankets, or medical supplies. And there was no place for them to go. Washington, D.C., as the nation's capital, was a bustling city, full of monuments, historic buildings, and important government offices. There were, however, no hospitals or military bases to send the soldiers to. Seeing the desperate need, Barton went to work. She took the most severely wounded to her sister's home in the city. Others were housed in whatever space was available, including the Senate chamber in the Capitol building. The next day, Barton packed up every useful item she could find: "sewing utensils, thread, needles, thimbles,

This photograph of Barton was taken during the Civil War era, a time in which she devoted herself to helping Union soldiers.

scissors, pens, buttons, strings, salves, tallow. . . ." She tore old bedsheets into strips for bandages, towels, and handkerchiefs. She went to every grocer in the neighborhood, asking them to donate food. She even hired a group of servants to help her carry all of the provisions to the troops at the Capitol. When Barton arrived in the Senate chamber, her former students crowded around her. Homesick, they were thrilled to see a friendly and familiar face. They also wanted to hear the latest news. Barton had only one copy of the newspaper, so she sat in the Senate president's seat and read it aloud to them.

From that moment on, Barton devoted all of her time and energy to caring for "her boys." She thrived on the challenge. She liked to accomplish things that others thought impossible, and she cared deeply for hurting people. War did not frighten Barton—it excited her. As a little girl, Barton always loved to hear her father's war stories. Captain

Barton had taught Clara that "next to Heaven our highest duty was to . . . serve our country and . . . support its laws." This was Clara's opportunity to step up and bravely serve her country. She would do it with passion, conviction, and determination.

In the next few weeks, more than 75,000 soldiers made their way to Washington, D.C. The arrival of more troops brought even more excitement. Barton wrote to her father, "I don't know how long it has been since my ear has been free from the roll of a drum, it is the music I sleep by, and I love it." The troops from New Jersey and New York included many of Barton's old friends and former students. Barton visited them

No Experience Necessary

In the 1800s, anyone could be a nurse. It was not a profession that required any special skill or formal training. When faced with illness or injury, family members frequently cared for each other, just as Barton cared for her brother David. Many "professional" nurses were little more than servants who took care of the sick when family members were unwilling or unable to do so. For the most part, these nurses simply watched over the patients, feeding them, bathing them, and changing their bandages. Some administered medication or assisted doctors in surgery. There were few hospitals. Doctors usually traveled to treat patients in their own homes. Out on the battlefield, where women were not allowed, all of the nurses were male soldiers. Back home, in the community, nurses were often female.

often. Whenever she could, she brought pies, cakes, and other home-made treats.

UNEXPECTED HELP

The troops still suffered from a shortage of basic supplies. Somehow, their families heard about Clara Barton and her work. They began sending food and clothing directly to her, instead of to the army. They hoped Barton would be able to locate their family members more quickly. Others simply wanted to donate something to the war effort. They thought Barton would know where it was needed. Barton received so many boxes of supplies that she had to move to a bigger apartment just to hold them all. She lived among an ever-growing mound of cartons, crates, and barrels. It took every spare moment to distribute the supplies.

Some people said that the city of Washington would soon be attacked. They moved farther north for safety. Not Barton. "I will remain here while anyone remains and do whatever comes to my hand," she said. "I may be compelled to face danger, but never fear it, and while our soldiers can stand and fight, I can stand and feed and nurse them."

As the Civil War got underway, the makeshift hospitals were soon filled to overflowing with wounded men. Barton visited patients daily, nursing them with all the compassion and care she had given her brother David years before. She tenderly held the soldiers' hands and offered words of encouragement. She fed those who were too weak to feed themselves and helped others write letters to their families. She brought the men combs, handkerchiefs, and other small comfort items.

Barton saw that many of the wounded men had been neglected on the battlefield, left for hours to starve or die of their wounds. They received no treatment until they were taken to the hospital. By that time, they had come down with infections and diseases. The hospitals constantly

Barton and other volunteers cared for wounded soldiers.

ran out of supplies. There were not enough doctors and nurses to care for all the wounded. Barton felt she had to do more.

She asked officers to tell her what the soldiers needed most. Then she wrote to all of her friends, asking them to contribute to the war effort. She put advertisements in the newspapers, urging women everywhere to prepare and send supplies. Always organized, Barton instructed them in the best way to package and ship different items. Almost every day, she spent her own money to buy the men fresh bread and whatever else they needed.

The response to Barton's request was overwhelming. People sent thousands and thousands of boxes full of much-needed items, such as clothing, fruit, tobacco, and soap. Barton had to rent space in three warehouses to hold all of the supplies. Every spare moment was consumed by her distribution duties.

As the war continued, Barton grew more and more concerned about the needs of the soldiers on the battlefields. Great numbers had died of simple infections and minor wounds because they were not treated quickly enough. Supplies were an even greater problem at the front. Barton knew she could help if she were allowed, but women were not allowed anywhere near the battlefield.

AN UNLIKELY ANGEL

Barton tried everything she could think of to get permission to go to the battlefield. She spoke to doctors and generals, governors and senators. She

A Father's Advice

During the war, Barton traveled to North Oxford to visit her father. Captain Barton was very ill and would not live much longer. Barton sat beside her father's bed. They talked about the war for hours. Clara asked her father what he thought of her desire to serve on the battlefront. People said no respectable woman would go there. Captain Barton dismissed their concerns. He challenged his daughter to serve her country with everything she had, even if it cost her life. He said she must always "honor God and love mankind" by doing whatever she could to find and comfort those in distress. Clara never forgot her father's advice.

begged to be allowed to take much-needed supplies to the front. But time after time, she was refused. The officers told her that a woman did not belong on a battlefield. It was too dangerous. She would be a distraction. She would get in the way. Instead of Barton taking care of soldiers, soldiers would end up taking care of *her*.

In spite of their discouragement, Barton would not give up or go away. She kept asking. In the summer of 1862, she finally got her chance. Colonel Daniel Rucker agreed to let her take supplies to the troops in Fredericksburg, Virginia. He even provided six wagons and drivers to transport them.

At Fredericksburg, Barton experienced the horrors of war first-hand. She stood on the battlefield where two thousand men lay dead and thousands more were dying. Some were bleeding to death. Others battled sunstroke and dehydration. She heard men shrieking in agony,

With little hesitation, Barton went out onto the battlefield to tend to the injured.

groaning in pain, and sobbing for help. Barton felt a wave of panic break over her. For a moment, she was paralyzed by fear. Then she gathered up her courage and went to work.

Out on the field, Barton whispered words of comfort as she held wounded men in her arms. She brought them water and treated their injuries as best she could. Back at the camp, Barton unloaded blankets, food, and medicine from the wagons. She cooked hot meals, applied bandages, and assisted doctors in surgery. Hour after hour, she worked tirelessly to ease the pain and suffering all around her. It was often gruesome work.

"I wrung the blood from the bottom of my clothing before I could step, for the weight about my feet," she told her friends. Barton witnessed unspeakable horrors, fields of blood, and bodies blown apart. It only strengthened her resolve to do more. She marched fearlessly into the fray, often risking her own life to save others.

At the Battle of Antietam, she used a pocketknife to remove a bullet from the jaw of one young soldier. She gently lifted another man's head to give him a drink of water. Just then, a bullet went through the sleeve of her dress and killed the man. Barton moved on until she found another soldier who—strangely—refused treatment for his wounds. Barton soon realized that the soldier was a young woman, Mary Calloway. Although it was against the law, Calloway had disguised herself as a man so that she could serve her country in the war. Barton understood that desire all too well. She protected Calloway's identity and helped her get to the hospital in Washington, where her sweetheart lay wounded. Both soldiers recovered from their injuries. They later married and named their oldest daughter after Clara.

By then, Barton had been given a new name. Thousands of grateful soldiers called her "the angel of the battlefield." Forty-year-old Barton made an unusual-looking angel. The hem of her blood-soaked skirt was pinned up around her waist. Her hair fell out of its bun and across her face, which was often smudged blue with gunpowder. But to the weary and wounded, Clara Barton was a heavenly sight.

Thousands of soldiers on both sides of the conflict died in the Battle of Antietam.

THE ANGELS OF THE BATTLE-FIELD.

Barton was regarded as a heroine for her actions during the Civil War.

FOUR

Recovering From War

When Clara Barton arrived at a temporary hospital near the battlefield, one of the doctors cried out, "The Lord has remembered us; you are here again!" There was something comforting about her presence. No matter how she felt inside, Barton always appeared calm and in control. She surveyed the situation and then cheerfully went to work, putting things in order and organizing the most effective system for distributing supplies. With the officers and doctors, Barton used a businesslike tone. She took charge. But with the wounded, Barton was gentle and kind. In all the turmoil and confusion, she made time to talk to each soldier personally. The men felt loved and cared for.

Surgeon James Dunn told his wife, "In my feeble estimation, General McClellan with all his laurels, sinks into insignificance beside the true heroine of the age, the angel of the battlefield."

As the Civil War continued, the army became more organized and better supplied. The War Board was the government agency in charge of supervising and coordinating the war on the home front. It handled financial matters, ordering equipment and supplies for the troops. It created policies and procedures for the army to follow. The War Board appointed a woman named Dorothea Dix to create the official Department of Women Nurses. At age fifty-nine, Dix was well known for her compassion for the needy and her concern for those neglected by society. She had worked tirelessly to promote better prison conditions and to improve the treatment of people who suffered from mental illness. Thanks to Clara Barton, the army had realized the value of women in the war effort. Now Dix would be in charge of developing a capable corps of professional nurses to serve the armed forces.

There were a number of other government agencies and volunteer associations that sought to improve conditions in the army. Barton avoided working with any of these groups. She often disagreed with their methods and ideas. Barton was convinced that her way was the best way. She preferred to be independent and did not want anyone else telling her what to do. Barton discovered that many of the female volunteers turned out to be distractions and nuisances—just as the officers had predicted. These women got sick at the sight of blood. They flirted with the soldiers and competed for their attention. Barton had no time for that sort of nonsense.

Sometimes, Barton's "take charge" manner offended other aid workers. Barton could be very stubborn. She resented it when people challenged her methods or questioned her motives. Some of the officers and volunteers complained that Barton was difficult to work with. Their criticism stung Barton. In some situations, she angrily defended herself against what she considered unjust accusations. At other times, she physically collapsed from anxiety and stress. But whenever someone needed her, Barton quickly rose to the occasion.

A NEW MISSION

In 1865, the Civil War ended. Many soldiers were still missing in action, and no one knew what had happened to them. Were they dead? Wounded? In prison camps? Families wrote to Barton to ask if she remembered seeing their loved ones on the battlefield or in hospitals. Barton couldn't resist their cries for help. She had to do something for them. She convinced President Lincoln to give her an office in the War Department. The president then issued a special announcement:

> To the Friends of Missing Persons
>
> Miss Clara Barton has kindly offered to search for the missing prisoners of war. Please address her at Annapolis, giving her [the] name, regiment, and company of any missing prisoner.
>
> Signed,
> A. Lincoln

For the next four years, Barton undertook the massive job of reuniting soldiers with their families. She studied the thousands and thousands of letters she received. Barton compiled lists of missing soldiers. She published them in newspapers and posted them in military hospitals, asking anyone with information about the missing men to contact her directly. Then Barton carefully sorted through the replies and forwarded information to the families. It was hard work, and Barton received no salary. She paid her office expenses out of her own pocket. Later, Senator Wilson saw to it that Congress reimburse Barton for at least some of the money she had spent.

One day, a young man named Dorence Atwater came to visit Barton. He told her an amazing story. As a Union soldier, he had been held captive by Confederate forces at the notorious prison in Andersonville. During the war, the prison held as many as 25,000 soldiers at a time. Many of them starved to death. Others were tortured. Illness and disease

After the war, Barton again sought to help soldiers. This time she wanted to help the ones that went missing during the conflict.

went untreated. When his jailors found out that Atwater had good hand-writing, they put him in charge of making a list of all the soldiers who died in the prison. These men were then buried in unmarked graves. Confederate officers kept detailed records for their own use, but they did not attempt to contact the families of the dead soldiers.

Thinking of these poor families, Atwater secretly made a copy of the list. He hid it in the lining of his coat. He also took notes about where each soldier was buried. Now that the war had ended, Atwater hoped his list could be used to help the families of the missing men. He wanted everyone to know what had happened at Andersonville. Atwater was not convinced that army officials would take the proper time and effort to contact families, so he presented another copy of his list to Barton. Barton looked over the list in shock and disbelief. There were almost 14,000 names on it. Barton felt the horror and tragedy of the war all over again.

With Dorence Atwater as her secretary and assistant, Barton traveled to the Andersonville prison. There, along with Captain James B. Moore, she supervised the difficult task of identifying and marking at least 13,000 graves.

BARTON TAKES THE STAGE

People all over the world had heard about the angel of the battlefield. Barton's bravery and compassion were legendary. Veterans of the Civil War raved about her. Barton received invitations to speak about her experiences to audiences around the country. The thought of speaking to large groups of people made Barton sick to her stomach. In some ways, she was still very shy. But the invitations kept coming. They were opportunities to tell her story and educate people about the realities of

This is the Andersonville National Cemetery where Barton worked to identify and mark the graves of thousands of soldiers who died in the Andersonville Prison. Today, the cemetery is part of the Andersonville National Historic Site.

war. Public speakers were also paid well, and Barton could use the money to replenish her depleted bank account.

Barton prepared a series of talks with titles such as "How the Republic Was Saved—or War Without the Tinsel," "Scenes of the Battlefield," and "Work and Incidents of War." In spite of her stage fright, Barton turned out to be a powerful speaker. She fascinated audiences with her vivid descriptions of the things she had witnessed on the battlefield. She told moving stories of bravery and sacrifice. Of all the popular lecturers at the time, she was the only one who had actually seen

A Day of Remembrance

In the years after the Civil War, the United States struggled to heal itself and rebuild the nation. People looked for ways to remember those who had died. Some wrote poems and songs about the war heroes, while others wore ribbons or flowers as symbols of mourning. Across the country, communities set aside different days to honor their dead. They decorated the soldiers' graves with flowers or flags.

In 1868, Senator John A. Logan announced that May 30 had been chosen as the date for a nationwide "memorial day." Still, it would not become an official holiday for more than one hundred years. In 1971, Congress declared Memorial Day a national holiday "to be celebrated on the last Monday in May." It began as a way to remember those who had died in the Civil War, but ever since World War I, people have set aside Memorial Day to honor those who have died in all of the wars fought by the United States.

action in the war. She could speak with authority and provide eyewitness accounts of famous battles and events.

As she traveled the lecture circuit, Barton met many other prominent women of her day, including feminists Frances Gage, Julia Ward Howe, Elizabeth Cady Stanton, and Susan B. Anthony. These women urged Barton to join them and voice support for women's rights. From time to time, Barton did speak out about the injustices she had suffered as a woman in a "male-dominated society." She praised the efforts of Anthony and the others, who were trying to persuade the government to give women the right to vote. But when it came to fully supporting the feminist movement, Barton stopped short. There were some things more important to her than crusading for women's rights.

Barton explained, "When I stood month after month and year after year among the wounded and slain *men* of my nation . . . I forgot in the great privilege of going to minister to their wants that any privileges had ever been denied me. I forgot that I was a woman. When

This note is a part of one of Barton's lectures.

I was strong — and I thought I ought to go to the rescue of the men who fell —:

But I struggled long and hard with my sense of propriety — with the appalling fact — that I was only a woman, whispering in one ear — and the groans of suffering men, dying like dogs — unfed and unsheltered, for the life of the very Institutions which had protected and educated me — thundering in the other —

—— I said that I struggled with my sense of propriety — and I say it with humiliation and shame — Before God and Before you I am ashamed that I thought of such a thing —

But when our armies fought a Cedar Mountain I Broke the shackles and went to the field

I raised the flag on 13,000 sleeping martyrs of Andersonville, I forgot that I could not vote."

At a conference in 1868, Barton told the audience that the movement to restore basic human rights to African American slaves should be a priority. "No person in this house could be more rejoiced than myself if it could be decided to admit at the same moment to a voice in the Government all persons and classes naturally and properly entitled to it. . . . But if the door be not wide enough to admit us all at once—and one must wait—then I am willing. I am willing to stand back and see the old, scared limping slave clank his broken fetters through before me—while I stand back with head uncovered—thanking God for his release."

From 1866 to 1868, Barton spoke more than three hundred times. She became a national celebrity. The people of the United States lovingly called her a "great war heroine."

The Lecture Circuit

In the days before radio, television, and the Internet, the lecture circuit was a popular source of entertainment and education. People attended lectures or speeches given by famous authors, politicians, scientists, and philosophers. It was often their only opportunity to see these newsmakers in person—to know what they looked like and how they sounded. Other popular speakers in Barton's day included Mark Twain, Ralph Waldo Emerson, and Susan B. Anthony.

Meeting Dr. Louis Appia would be a life-changing event for Barton.

TIME TO REST

In 1869, the years of intense and emotionally draining work finally caught up with Barton. She was exhausted. In Boston one night, she opened her mouth to begin her talk, only to discover that she could not speak. At the advice of her doctors, Barton immediately canceled her remaining speaking engagements. For the sake of her health, she traveled to Europe to spend time resting and relaxing. After touring England and France, Barton arrived in Geneva, Switzerland. There she met a doctor named Louis Appia. He wanted to talk with the "angel of the battlefield." Their meeting would change Barton's life forever.

Appia was a member of the International Red Cross. The Red Cross had been founded in 1863 by a Swiss banker, Jean Henri Dunant. Years before, Dunant witnessed the suffering of the more than forty thousand soldiers wounded in battle at Solferino, Italy. Filled with grief and compassion, Dunant rounded up the local townspeople and led them out onto the battlefield. They bandaged wounds and provided food and water to injured soldiers on both sides of the war. When he returned to Switzerland, Dunant wrote a book about his experience called *A Memory of Solferino*. He called for the creation of national relief societies. The societies would prepare and train volunteers in first aid during peacetime so they would be ready to assist the wounded in times of war.

At the Geneva Convention in 1864, representatives from sixteen countries agreed on guidelines for the humane treatment of prisoners of war. The International Committee of the Red Cross was established as a neutral and independent relief society. The society would provide aid and assistance to all those wounded in war, no matter which side they were on. The society chose the symbol of a plain red cross on a white background. Volunteers wore armbands with the Red Cross symbol to protect them from being mistaken for enemy soldiers. Armies would be told not to shoot at Red Cross relief workers.

Barton could not believe that she had never even heard of this organization. She thought that it was an incredible idea and a wonderful way to help the wounded. Appia gave her an armful of books and pamphlets that described the work of the Red Cross. He explained that, although thirty-two countries had joined the Geneva Convention, the United States government had refused to participate. Government representatives would not sign the Treaty of Geneva. This amazed Barton. She couldn't imagine why the government wouldn't want to participate in such a valuable, life-saving organization.

Barton told Appia just what he had hoped to hear: She would go back to the United States and speak to her friends in the Senate. She would find out why the United States refused to join the Red Cross and would convince them to change their minds. This was a perfect job for Clara Barton.

The Two Famous Nurses Never Met

People often called Clara Barton "the American Florence Nightingale." Florence Nightingale achieved fame as the founder of modern nursing. Like Barton, she cared deeply for suffering people, especially those in the military. During the Crimean War (1853–1856), Nightingale tended to thousands of wounded men on the battlefields and in English army hospitals. She opened the world's first school of nursing to train people in the profession.

Barton and Nightingale lived at the same time and shared many of the same passions and concerns. But although they exchanged a few polite notes, they never met—not even when Barton stayed in London, just a few blocks away from Nightingale's house. Historians suspect that because both women fought so hard to earn respect and recognition in their field, neither one cared to share the spotlight with the other.

FIVE

The Birth of a New Dream

Before Clara Barton could return to the United States, war broke out between France and Prussia (Germany). The Prussian chancellor, Otto von Bismarck, had been plotting to combine all of the individual German states into a unified German empire. The people of France felt threatened by his efforts, believing correctly that Bismarck intended to attack and conquer their nation next. In 1870, France declared war on Prussia. The French were defeated by the Germans the following year.

During this conflict, Barton witnessed the Red Cross in action as she joined their relief efforts in Switzerland. She was amazed by the society's efficiency. Barton later said, "I saw the work of these Red Cross societies in the field, accomplishing in four months under this systematic organization what we failed to accomplish in four years without it—no mistakes, no needless suffering, no starving, no lack of care, no waste, no confusion, but order, plenty, cleanliness, and comfort whenever that little flag made its way, a whole continent marshaled under the banner of the Red Cross—as I saw all this, and joined and worked in it, you would not wonder that I said to myself, 'If I live to return to my country, I will try to make my people understand the Red Cross and that treaty.'"

At first, Barton stayed in Switzerland, making bandages to replenish the supplies in the Red Cross warehouse. But just as she had before, Barton longed to be on the battlefield, caring for the wounded and serving where the need was greatest. Barton received permission to accompany a young Swiss woman, Antoinette Margot, who was driving a wagonload of supplies to the battlefront. As they traveled through the French countryside, Barton realized for the first time the devastating effects of war on civilians. Towns and villages had been destroyed by enemy troops. Entire families were left without food or shelter. Just like wounded soldiers, many of them battled starvation and disease. Together with other volunteers, Barton set up centers for the distribution of food and clothing. Barton was especially moved by the plight of the young women. Orphaned or widowed, they had no way to earn a living and support themselves.

After giving it some thought, Barton came up with a creative way to provide for the destitute women of Prussia. She believed it was better to teach people to help themselves than to just give them a handout.

With financial support from the Grand Duchess Louise of Baden, Barton opened a sewing room. In this room, needy women could pick up the materials necessary for sewing various items of clothing. They worked at home. When they finished the clothing, they brought it back to the sewing room. They were paid a small wage for each day's work, and the clothes were distributed to victims of the war. In Barton's sewing program, the women not only earned a living, but also contributed to their community in a valuable way.

The sewing room was a tremendous success. It employed up to three hundred women at a time. The citizens of Strasbourg appreciated Barton's efforts. They thanked her for bringing a spirit of courage and hope to their people. The emperor and empress of Germany awarded Barton the Iron Cross of Merit. The grand duke and duchess of Baden presented her with the Gold Cross of Remembrance. Later, Barton

This illustration shows Barton entering Strasbourg with the Germany army.

traveled to Paris to take first-aid supplies and to work with the city's homeless.

As the war ended, Barton continued her tour of the historic sites of Europe. Friends and family came to visit her in Europe, including her sister Sally, Senator Wilson, and Dorence Atwater. Barton attended parties and receptions. She met with famous and influential people. She even saw Dr. L. N. Fowler in London. He was the man who, years earlier, suggested to her parents that Barton begin a career in teaching.

After three years in Europe, Barton prepared to return home. She had already started to show signs of exhaustion and illness. Dark days lay ahead for Barton.

An Artist at Heart

Clara Barton loved nothing more than a good challenge. She worked well under pressure. As a teacher, a clerk, and a nurse, she was drawn to the most difficult tasks, the toughest problems. For rest and relaxation, she chose activities that gave her an outlet for creative expression. Barton crafted beautiful quilts, drew pictures of local scenery, and wrote poems about her feelings and experiences. At the Andersonville prison, where she helped mark 13,000 graves, Barton wrote:

> *Well, Mothers I am here—here with your darling ones*
> *Before me lie the narrow graves that hold your martyred sons*
> *And sisters pale with weeping close clasp one another*
> *Here lies the tribute wreath I've turned for that lost and noble brother.*

A SEASON OF SUFFERING

When Barton left Europe in 1873, her friends said good-bye at a lavish party in her honor. When she arrived in the United States, the citizens of North Oxford lined the streets to welcome back their hometown hero. Compared to most women of her day, Clara Barton had lived an extraordinary life. She was well educated and widely experienced. She had been a successful teacher and a successful businesswoman. In wartime, she single-handedly saved thousands of lives and brought comfort to thousands more. She was internationally recognized for her humanitarian efforts. Barton counted some of the most famous and influential people in the world as her personal friends. Thanks to her success on the lecture circuit, she was financially secure.

In spite of this, Barton often struggled with insecurity and self-doubt. She worried about what other people thought of her. She desperately needed their approval and respect. For some reason, Barton often felt unwanted and unloved. When these feelings came to the surface, she grew terribly depressed. Her emotional distress affected her physical health. For years, she battled health problems that doctors couldn't diagnose or cure. These physical problems led to even greater depression and anxiety. Sometimes, Barton simply worked too hard. She tried to do too much.

When Barton returned home from Europe, she suffered a total nervous breakdown. She was confined to her bed for the next two years, unable to see, talk, or move. She wouldn't eat. She couldn't sleep. She just lay in her bed, crying hysterically. Not surprisingly, Barton started losing weight. Her dark hair turned completely white. Doctors could do nothing to help her. Barton's friends were gravely concerned.

A SLOW RECOVERY

A friend from Switzerland came to stay with Barton and nurse her back to health. In time, Barton showed signs of improving. By the fall of 1874, she could sit up in bed and even sketch a little. Six months later, she was able to dress herself, write a few letters, and do some sewing. But she refused all visitors and rarely left her room. Barton was still deeply depressed.

In March of 1876, Barton decided to visit "Our Home on the Hillside," a health center run by Dr. James Jackson in Dansville, New York. The facilities were located in a beautiful area surrounded by rolling hills and leafy trees. It was a very peaceful environment. Jackson correctly believed that many popular medicines were actually harmful to patients. Instead, he emphasized a healthy diet of whole grains, fresh fruits, and vegetables. Patients were encouraged to dress comfortably and get plenty of fresh air and exercise. Jackson insisted that they maintain a positive attitude about their recovery. He brought in popular speakers, reformers such as women's rights activist Susan B. Anthony, and former slaves turned abolitionists such as Frederick Douglass and Sojourner Truth. Their lectures were inspiring. Rest, relaxation, and encouragement—it was just what Barton needed.

At Jackson's health center, Barton grew stronger each day. She learned to pace herself and to not try to do too much. Barton adopted the healthier lifestyle Jackson recommended. She never again suffered such a serious breakdown.

Still struggling with her depression, Barton sought help at a health center in Dansville, New York.

READY FOR WORK

By 1877, Barton's recovery was complete. She felt ready and eager to get back to work. At the age of fifty-six, she still had many good years ahead of her. Once again, she began looking for a way to use her skills to help others. War broke out between Russia and Turkey. As Barton heard reports of the conflict, memories of her own battleground experiences came flooding back.

"Like the old war horse that has rested long in quiet pastures, I recognize the bugle note that calls me to my place," she said. "Though I may not do what I once could, I am come to offer what I may."

Anxious to help, Barton wondered if she could get U.S. citizens to donate supplies for the relief of the wounded. Barton remembered her

A Full House

Barton's compassion extended to anyone in need—the sick, wounded, abandoned, destitute—and very often, her own poorer relatives. In addition to nursing the sick, Barton offered comfort and advice to those who were discouraged. She provided financial aid to those who were unemployed or overcome by debt. In her later years, Barton's house was always full of friends and relatives whom she generously supported. Sometimes they relied too heavily on Barton and took advantage of her kindness. But Barton never tired of giving to those in need.

promise to Appia in Switzerland. She wrote a letter, asking him if she could start an American Red Cross Society.

A NEW DREAM

Appia was delighted to receive Barton's letter. He immediately contacted Gustave Moynier, the president of the International Committee of the Red Cross. The leadership committee decided to appoint Barton as its official representative to Washington. She would be responsible for educating the U.S. government about the work of the Red Cross. She would also raise public awareness and support for the Treaty of Geneva and its policies concerning the fair treatment of prisoners of war.

As she told Appia, "the knowledge of your Society and its great objects in this country . . . is almost unknown and the Red Cross, in America, is a mystery."

It was an important first step in the process of organizing an American Red Cross Society. Barton would devote the rest of her life to this dream. One day, it would stand as her greatest accomplishment.

Barton couldn't wait to get going on her new job. She began preparations for a journey to Washington.

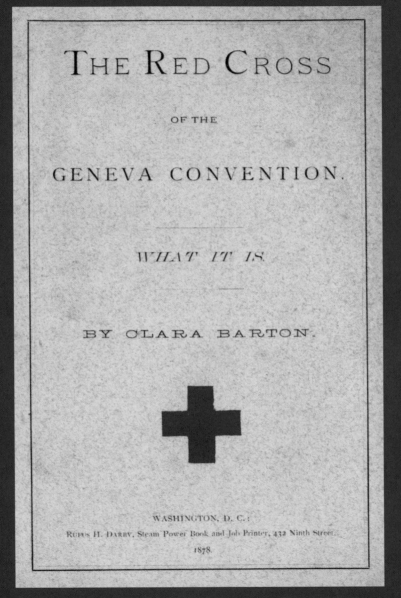

THE RED CROSS

OF THE

GENEVA CONVENTION.

WHAT IT IS.

BY CLARA BARTON.

WASHINGTON, D. C.:
RUFUS H. DARBY, Steam Power Book and Job Printer, 432 Ninth Street.
1878.

Barton wrote this booklet to help convince U.S. political figures to let her form an American Red Cross Society.

SIX

A Different Kind of Battle

Bringing the Red Cross to the United States turned out to be the biggest battle of Clara Barton's life. She talked to doctors, lawyers, and Civil War veterans. She met with congressmen and cabinet members. Though they listened politely when Barton spoke, they expressed no interest in creating an American Red Cross Society. Most people believed that the United States would never again experience war. They didn't see any use for the Red Cross in peacetime. Many political leaders thought it was dangerous for the United States to join an international society. It might give other countries an opportunity to interfere with the U.S. government and its policies.

To answer these concerns, Barton wrote a booklet called "The Red Cross of the Geneva Convention: What It Is." She explained that the

Treaty of Geneva was not designed to control or influence foreign governments in political matters. It simply provided guidelines for the fair and humane treatment of prisoners of war. And it specified that doctors, nurses, and volunteers who treated the wounded should be considered neutral aid workers, not enemies to either side of those in conflict. Soldiers were to be instructed not to harm those who wore the symbol of the Red Cross.

In the same booklet, Barton pointed out that the Red Cross could be of great help in peacetime by providing relief to victims of "national or widespread calamities, such as plague . . . devastating fires or floods, railroad disasters, mining catastrophes, etc."

IMPORTANT MEETINGS

Barton wrote many other booklets, pamphlets, and newspaper articles about the work of the Red Cross. She mentioned it in interviews and speeches. In January of 1878, Barton went to the White House to meet with President Rutherford B. Hayes. She took with her a letter written by Gustave Moynier, the president of the International Red Cross. In the letter, Moynier urged President Hayes to recognize the invaluable service that the Red Cross could render to those in need and to sign the Treaty of Geneva.

President Hayes told Barton that she needed to discuss the matter with Secretary William Evarts of the State Department, so Barton arranged a meeting at his office. Secretary Evarts referred Barton to another official,

Frederick Seward. Seward's father had rejected the idea of cooperating with the Geneva Convention years before. Seward did the same. He told Barton in no uncertain terms that the United States would not sign a treaty that required it to submit to laws created in another country.

"It is all settled," Seward said. "The question will never be considered again."

BIDING HER TIME

Barton was terribly discouraged by the resistance to the Red Cross, but she refused to give up. She wrote a letter to Appia describing the results of her meetings in Washington. "With that previous refusal in the way[,] it will require great care, labor, and perseverance to gain the point desired, but I shall not despair until I must."

Barton spoke about the Red Cross to everyone she met. She enlisted the help of her friends to spread the word. Several influential newspaper editors

Barton even spoke with President Rutherford B. Hayes in her efforts to create the American Red Cross Society.

The Monroe Doctrine

Many government officials refused Clara Barton's Red Cross proposal because they believed that signing the Treaty of Geneva would violate the Monroe Doctrine. The Monroe Doctrine was a policy established by President James Monroe. It stated that European countries did not have the right to influence or control countries in the Western Hemisphere and that the United States would not attempt to interfere in European affairs. Having fought a revolution to be free and independent, most U.S. citizens were reluctant to form close associations with other countries. In his farewell address in 1796, President George Washington had warned U.S. citizens against "permanent alliances with foreign nations."

took up the cause. They helped Barton publish numerous articles and news reports to educate the public about the work of the Red Cross. Barton believed that if the American people supported it, the government would have to recognize and accept the Treaty of Geneva and the International Committee of the Red Cross.

Barton worked tirelessly to promote the society. She wrote another, longer pamphlet and printed five thousand copies to distribute.

Barton campaigned tirelessly to get the word out about the Treaty of Geneva and the Red Cross.

She paid for this project with her own money. Barton decided to go ahead and organize the American Red Cross Society, even though it was not yet officially approved by the government or the International Red Cross. Barton hoped to have the opportunity to demonstrate the usefulness of the society so people would understand its value. In 1881, forest fires destroyed thousands of homes in Michigan. Barton and her Red Cross volunteers raised $80,000 for the relief effort. They sent cases of medicines, clothing, and tools.

Barton's campaign proved very effective. She discovered that, once again, she had friends in high places. A new president sat in the Oval Office at the White House. Unlike President Hayes, President James A. Garfield enthusiastically supported the idea of an American Red Cross Society. So did Secretary of State James Blaine and Senator Omar D. Conger. Together, they worked swiftly to bring the Treaty of Geneva to the attention of the Senate.

DISASTER AND DELAY

Just when it seemed that Barton's dream had finally come true, disaster struck. In July of 1881, President Garfield became the victim of an assassination attempt. Doctors tried to revive him, but he was unable to recover from his gunshot wounds. After lying in a coma for almost two months, President Garfield died. Vice President Chester Arthur then took charge of the country. As the new president, he had many urgent matters to attend to.

Barton was deeply saddened by the death of President Garfield, and she had no idea whether President Arthur supported the Geneva Convention. She did not know if Arthur favored the idea of the Red Cross or if he even knew about it. She worried that she would have to start her campaign all over again. To her great relief, Barton found that President Arthur did know about the Red Cross. Just like President Garfield, he supported the idea. To Barton's great joy and delight, President Arthur signed the Treaty of Geneva on March 1, 1882. He urged the U.S. Senate

This photograph shows President Arthur's signature on the Treaty of Geneva.

Barton Goes to Jail

Right in the middle of her efforts to bring the Red Cross to the United States, Barton received an urgent request from Governor Benjamin Butler. During the Civil War, Butler had often helped Barton get past official regulations and political barriers to gain access to the battlefield. Now, he desperately needed someone to take over the Massachusetts Reformatory Prison for Women. Although she hated the thought, Barton could not say no.

For six months she served as prison superintendent. She renovated the buildings and reorganized the administration. She invited prisoners to share suggestions, requests, or complaints, and she responded to every one. Barton always treated the women with compassion and respect. She did everything she could to help them improve their lives and find hope for the future.

to ratify it quickly. According to the Constitution, the Senate had to approve any treaties the president signed. Barton was invited to testify about the Red Cross before the Senate Foreign Relations Committee. She told them all about this wonderful international society. On March 16, the Senate gave their full approval. They ratified the Treaty of Geneva, making it possible for the United States to officially join the International Red Cross Society.

It was a historic moment and an incredible accomplishment. All the credit went to Clara Barton. For years, she had labored to bring this to pass. There were cheers heard around the world, as the International Committee of the Red Cross welcomed the United States of America as its newest member.

In 1884, Barton's dreams of the American Red Cross Society came true.

MADAM PRESIDENT

Clara Barton was unanimously elected president of the American Red Cross Society. In September of 1884, Barton traveled to Geneva, Switzerland, to attend the Third International Conference of the Red Cross. She became the first woman ever to officially represent the U.S. government at an international conference. The convention hosted eighty-five delegates from twenty-two countries. Barton was the only female delegate.

Barton was honored at parties and receptions all over the city of Geneva. Everywhere she went, people greeted her with thunderous applause. Everyone wanted to talk to the famous Clara Barton. They sought her opinions and advice on a wide variety of topics. International Committee of the Red Cross officials treated Barton with the utmost respect and admiration.

Barton attended committee meetings and lectures. With great interest, she observed workshops on new surgical techniques, advanced first aid, and improvements in hospital and ambulance design. At a leadership council meeting, Barton introduced the "American Amendment" to the Treaty of Geneva. The amendment stated that in peacetime, the Red Cross should engage in humanitarian work, providing relief and assistance to victims of calamity and disaster, not just war.

Barton's experience at the conference thoroughly energized her. She couldn't wait to get home and get back to her work at the American Red Cross.

SEVEN

The Red Cross to the Rescue

For the next twenty years, Clara Barton dedicated herself to the work of the American Red Cross. Whenever disaster struck, duty called Barton to assist the unfortunate and relieve their suffering. Over and over, the Red Cross came to the rescue with Clara Barton leading the way.

In 1884, the Red Cross provided food, blankets, and clothing to the victims of the Ohio River flood. For three months, Barton and her assistants traveled up and down the river by boat, handing out supplies to needy families who lived far from the city shelters. They raised $175,000 in donations, which is equivalent to $3.2 million in today's money.

In Alabama and Louisiana, Barton and the Red Cross volunteers assisted tornado survivors. Later, on her way back from a speaking trip in California, Barton took $500 to aid victims of a massive earthquake in Charleston, South Carolina.

Next, Barton went to Eastland, Texas, where its citizens were suffering from a twenty-month drought. Barton had heard alarming reports of the devastation. She wanted to see it for herself. Barton reported on the terrible conditions to the Texas State Legislature. They approved a $100,000 donation (worth $1.8 million in today's money) to help the counties that were hardest hit. Barton contacted newspaper editors and asked them to publicize the drought and make people aware of the victims' ongoing needs.

More than thirty Red Cross nurses—male and female, black and white—traveled to Jacksonville, Florida, to treat an epidemic of yellow fever. At the time, no one knew this flulike virus was spread by mosquitoes. Thousands of people became ill, and many died. There were no remedies or treatments for yellow fever, but the Red Cross nurses provided comfort and care.

As more people recognized the tremendous work of the Red Cross, they decided to get involved in the organization. Branches, or chapters, of the Red Cross sprang up around the country. From New York to California, these chapters recruited volunteers and trained them in first aid and disaster relief. They reached out to those in need wherever they found them. The popularity of the Red Cross grew tremendously.

BARTON'S SHINING MOMENT

In May of 1889, heavy rains caused flooding in Johnstown, Pennsylvania. Above the city, a huge dam broke. A wall of water more than 30 feet (9.1 meters) high came crashing down the mountain. It destroyed everything in its path. Three thousand men, women, and children lost their lives.

After touring the area, Barton said, "I cannot lose the memory of that first walk on the first day. The wading in mud, the climbing over broken engines, cars, heaps of iron rollers, broken timbers, wrecks of houses, bent railway tracks, tangled with piles of iron wire, bands of workmen, squads of military—the getting around bodies of dead animals, and often people[,] . . . the smouldering fires, and drizzling rain."

Barton went into action at once, calling for volunteer workers, donations, and supplies. The Red Cross distributed boxes of food, medicine, and clothing. They provided kitchen utensils, simple furniture, and tools to help people rebuild their lives. With lumber donated by the state of Iowa, Red Cross volunteers built three large, temporary shelters for

The Johnstown flood caused great destruction, wrecking homes and businesses.

families who had lost their homes. The shelters were designed like hotels, with a separate room for each family and a large dining room and common area for social gatherings. To those who had been living in soggy tents or out in the open, it was a heavenly refuge.

Under Barton's direction, the Red Cross continued its work in the community all through the summer and into the fall. The organization not only provided for the town's physical needs, it offered comfort and encouragement as well. It lifted people's spirits and helped them get

Rescuing the Rough Riders

The Spanish-American War was fought in 1898 when the island of Cuba declared its independence from Spain. Spain responded with military force, and the United States was drawn into the conflict, fighting on behalf of Cuba. During the four-month war, Colonel Theodore Roosevelt led a volunteer regiment called the Rough Riders. Some of his men were wounded, and Roosevelt badly needed supplies to care for them. When he arrived at the Red Cross station in Cuba, Roosevelt asked the volunteers how much it would cost to purchase supplies. They informed him that their supplies weren't for sale—"not for a million dollars!"

Roosevelt was dismayed. He wondered aloud how he could possibly acquire the much-needed supplies for his men. A volunteer quickly explained, "Just ask for them, Colonel!" The Red Cross freely gave whatever it had. The future president walked away with everything he needed that day.

back on their feet. Barton led the way, playing a major role in the relief effort. The *Johnstown Daily Tribune* wrote about Barton: "Hunt the Dictionaries of all languages through and you will not find the signs to express our appreciation of her and her work. Try to describe the sunshine, try to describe the starlight. Words fail."

BARTON CARRIES ON

In 1893, Muslim Turkish soldiers massacred thousands of Armenian Christians in an attempt to rid their empire of the "troublesome" minority. Those who weren't killed by guns and swords were left in the ruins of their homes and villages. Many would die of starvation. Clara Barton herself traveled to Asia on behalf of the Red Cross to provide aid to the towns and villages destroyed by the conflict.

At the age of seventy-seven, Barton sailed to Cuba to distribute 600 tons of supplies during the Spanish-American War. She worked sixteen-hour days, organizing the relief effort and nursing the wounded. It brought back memories of her Civil War days. "I had not thought to ever make gruel again over a campfire," she said. "I never thought to see and take part in another war." But the United States had become entangled in Cuba's fight for independence from Spain. And as Barton observed, "Now that we are in it there is no way but to go through it."

On September 8, 1900, a powerful hurricane leveled the city of Galveston, Texas. Almost every home was destroyed, and as many as six thousand people were killed. Barton rushed to the scene. "It was naturally my work to go to that field," she later explained. With the help of Red Cross volunteers, Barton organized the creation of an orphanage, a soup kitchen, and a shelter for the homeless. For two months, aid workers stayed on the job in Galveston. They distributed donations of food, clothing, medicines, tools, and building materials. Before they left, Barton

The streets of Galveston were flooded because of the hurricane.

took 1.5 million strawberry plants to the farmers whose crops had been washed away in the storm.

As Barton got older, she showed no signs of slowing down. In fact, she purposely hid any signs of her advancing age. Though she could have used it, she refused help climbing into streetcars or getting up and down the stairs. No matter how tired she was, she insisted that she did not need rest. Barton wouldn't wear "old lady" clothes in the soft, muted colors that were popular with elderly women in her day. Instead, she wore bright red dresses with green sashes. She dyed her hair dark brown and wore plenty of makeup so that she would look as young as she felt.

TOO MUCH FOR ONE PERSON

Whenever duty called, Barton answered. She was the first one on the scene, always in the thick of the action. Unfortunately, her eagerness to be personally involved in every project led to serious problems for the Red Cross. It might have been better for Barton to concentrate on building the society itself. With Barton out on the field, there was no one to run the office and coordinate the efforts of the various chapters. The American Red Cross badly needed a capable staff of supervisors and administrators. This staff should have been setting policies and procedures for aid workers to follow. But, as always, Barton preferred being in charge of everything herself. She was convinced that no one could do the job any better than she could. She wouldn't even consider sharing her authority with anyone else. Barton ran the Red Cross as she saw fit.

She did not accept the suggestions or offers of help that came from board members and volunteers.

Many of these volunteers grew increasingly frustrated with Barton. They had ideas that would help the Red Cross grow and become even more effective in its work. Some of them thought that Barton was simply too old to run a national organization. A few said that Barton desired praise and recognition more than she desired helping people. She wouldn't accept help because she wanted all the credit for herself. Others accused Barton of mishandling Red Cross funds. Barton never did keep proper financial records.

In 1902, the attacks on Barton's character intensified. Hearing all of the rumors, President Theodore Roosevelt publicly questioned Barton's use of government funds. An influential woman named Mabel Boardman held an important position on the Red Cross Advisory Board. At first, Barton and Boardman shared a cordial respect for one another. But eventually, Boardman sided with Barton's critics and led the campaign against Barton. Boardman, clearly the next in line for leadership of the Red Cross, called for a formal investigation of the society's finances and demanded Barton's resignation.

BARTON FIGHTS BACK

Barton was shocked and outraged. She had given her life to the Red Cross. Perhaps she should have shared some of the responsibilities. She could have included others in her decision making. She also should have

Mabel Boardman

To Clara Barton, Mabel Boardman had become a bitter enemy. But Boardman was a lifesaver for the American Red Cross. She took over its leadership at a time when the society desperately needed to be strengthened and reorganized. Boardman established many new programs that emphasized training volunteers in first aid and lifesaving skills. Under her leadership, the Red Cross raised awareness of public health issues and raised money to help fight contagious diseases such as tuberculosis.

Unlike Barton, Boardman paid strict attention to accounting and financial matters. She surrounded herself with a carefully chosen and professionally trained staff that could share responsibility for the organization. But just like Barton, Boardman was clearly the boss. Both were courageous, powerful, and intelligent women. Both shared a lifelong passion for the American Red Cross. Mabel Boardman served the society she loved for more than forty years.

hired an accountant to run the business aspects or she should have at least saved her receipts! But Barton had never abused her authority. She had not been careless or irresponsible. She carefully evaluated every request for assistance and looked for the best way to use Red Cross funds. She never wasted a penny that had been donated to the society.

To say that she lived a life of luxury at the expense of the Red Cross, as some had whispered, was absolutely ridiculous. Barton had always lived simply, on her own resources. She never accepted a salary from the Red Cross. In fact, she spent thousands of dollars of her own money to establish the Red Cross and keep it running.

Barton's friends and supporters rallied around her. They wrote articles and booklets about her selfless contributions to the society and defended her against her opponents' attacks. With their help, Barton was able to retain the presidency of the Red Cross. After an official investigation of the society's finances, she was completely cleared of all the charges leveled against her. But Barton had been deeply wounded by the attacks. She never truly recovered. In 1904, at the age of eighty-three, Barton voluntarily resigned as president of the Red Cross. Mabel Boardman took over the leadership of the society. It was one of the bitterest days of Barton's life.

Clara Barton may have resigned from the American Red Cross, but she had no intention of retiring. In 1905, she founded the National First Aid Association of America. The organization was created to meet the needs of individual families affected by personal disaster. The First Aid Association assisted those who had lost their jobs or homes or suffered

This photograph of Barton's Glen Echo home was taken on the day that she resigned from the Red Cross.

Susan B. Anthony

When critics accused Clara Barton of mismanaging the Red Cross, Susan B. Anthony came quickly to her defense. Anthony was the president of the National Women's Suffrage Association and one of Barton's most outspoken supporters. The two had become good friends when they were both popular speakers on the lecture circuit after the Civil War.

A bright and articulate woman, Anthony was an international celebrity. She had dedicated her life to reforming society's wrongs, campaigning vigorously against the practice of slavery and the abuse of alcohol. But Anthony is best remembered for her passionate crusade for women's rights, particularly the right to vote.

from serious illness. Working for the association helped Barton keep her mind off her disastrous departure from the Red Cross. She was still an honorary member of the society, and she never stopped caring about its welfare. "It must grow," she said. "I want it to, it is my planting. I should rejoice the crop no matter who harvests it."

Leaving a Legacy

Barton continued to speak at conventions and conferences around the country. She even traveled to St. Petersburg, Russia, for the Seventh International Conference of the Red Cross. There, she gave a report on the efforts of the Red Cross during the Spanish-American War. In recognition of her service to the Russian people years earlier, Czar Nicholas II awarded Barton his nation's highest civilian honor, the Silver Cross of Imperial Russia. The Turkish government had already honored her with the "second order of Shekafet," an unusually large medal surrounded by diamonds and other precious jewels.

Clara Barton made headlines wherever she went. Reporters were eager to interview this "living legend." She received them graciously, happy to tell her stories of days gone by. Admirers longed for a glimpse of the famous "angel of the battlefield." They lined up to talk with her at parties and receptions. Whenever she could, Barton attended the many memorials and patriotic celebrations that honored Civil War veterans. She still referred to the aging soldiers as "her boys."

When Barton was asked to speak at feminist rallies, she expressed her confidence that women would soon be given the right to vote. "Man is trying to carry the burdens of the world alone," she said. "When he has the efficient help of woman he should be glad, and he will be. Just now it is new and strange, and men cannot comprehend what it would mean. But when such help comes, and men are used to it, they will be

The Right to Vote

For more than fifty years, women such as Susan B. Anthony and Elizabeth Cady Stanton devoted themselves to working for women's suffrage. They fought for the right of women to make their voices heard by voting in elections and participating in the government of their country. Unfortunately, these women did not live to see their dream come true.

As time went on, progress was made. Women were given more opportunities for education. More professional careers became available to them. They received better treatment under the law when it came to property rights, divorce, and child-custody issues. Society's standards of what was considered an acceptable or appropriate role for a woman had begun to change. But it wasn't until 1920 that Congress passed the Nineteenth Amendment to the Constitution, giving women the right to vote.

grateful for it. The change is not far away. This country is to know woman suffrage, and it will be a glad and proud day when it comes."

At the insistence of her friends, Barton wrote a number of books, including *The Red Cross in Peace and War* and *The Story of My Childhood*. Well into her eighties, she maintained an active lifestyle. Barton cooked, cleaned, and looked after herself at her home in Glen Echo, Maryland. She milked the cow, raked leaves, and shoveled snow. Once, she repainted the entire house by herself.

SEARCHING FOR SOMETHING MORE

In her later years, Barton explored different forms of spirituality. She had always believed in God. Her parents raised her as a member of the Universalist Church. As a young adult, Barton wrote that she respected the teachings of Jesus in the Bible. She admired his example of compassion for the poor and needy. But she had trouble understanding some of the doctrines of traditional Christian faith. She was drawn to the Christian Science movement and the teachings of its founder, Mary Baker Eddy. Eddy's ideas about self-healing appealed to Barton.

Barton had outlived many of her loved ones and was lonely. After the bitterness of her battle to retain control of the Red Cross, she needed comfort and encouragement. Barton looked for it wherever she could find it.

She experimented with the occult—rituals that claimed to connect a person to mysterious, supernatural powers. Barton attended séances,

In her later years, Barton explored spirituality and the occult.

ceremonies at which she believed she had spoken with the spirits of the dead. She thought she had received messages from old friends and family members, as well as historical figures such as President Lincoln and Kaiser Wilhelm I.

As time went on, Barton experienced a series of health problems. She came down with bronchitis repeatedly. Then a spinal injury kept her in bed for more than a year. In 1911, Barton became gravely ill with pneumonia. She seemed close to death. Well-wishers from around the world sent cards and prayers for her recovery. Somehow, Barton fought off the illness and managed to recover temporarily. Then, a few months after her ninetieth birthday, Barton became sick again. This time, Barton felt sure she would die. "They tell me I am changing worlds," she wrote

Medals and Flowers

Countries around the world honored Clara Barton for her service to humanity through the work of the Red Cross. They showered her with medals, ribbons, and jewels as tokens of their appreciation. These honors were very meaningful to Barton. She gave her life selflessly to others, but she constantly sought reassurance that she had truly made a difference. She needed to know that her efforts were appreciated.

When visitors arrived at her home in Glen Echo, they were often surprised to find the elderly Barton on her hands and knees in the garden. She was working in her flower beds, wearing a full array of medals and ribbons pinned to her chest.

to a friend. Barton prepared for her death by settling her business affairs and saying her good-byes. She spent her remaining weeks in bed, weak and heavily medicated. On the morning of April 12, 1912, Barton suddenly opened her eyes and cried out, "Let me go, let me go."

The next moment, she was gone.

AMERICA'S HEROINE

In her lifetime, Clara Barton overcame tremendous obstacles to achieve greatness. She struggled with fear, depression, and insecurity. She battled the expectations and limitations of a culture that didn't know what to make of a successful, independent woman. She experienced rejection, betrayal, and heartbreak. Through it all, Barton showed incredible courage and strength of character. She never lost sight of the things she believed in. Barton loved to tackle tough assignments; she enjoyed hard work. It made her success that much sweeter.

Millions of people owe their lives to Clara Barton and the work of the Red Cross. Today, the American Red Cross Society is the largest humanitarian organization in the United States. It functions with the aid of 1.2 million volunteers. There are 1,100 individual chapters of the Red Cross around the country. These chapters respond to 67,000 disasters each year, including floods, earthquakes, outbreaks of disease and illness, household fires, and transportation accidents. They also send assistance to as many as forty other countries around the globe. The society is the primary supplier of blood and blood products in the United States. In 2000, the Red Cross trained 12 million people in lifesaving skills.

When terrorists attacked the Pentagon and the World Trade Center on September 11, 2001, the American Red Cross responded immediately. It provided gallons of lifesaving blood for the injured, as well as

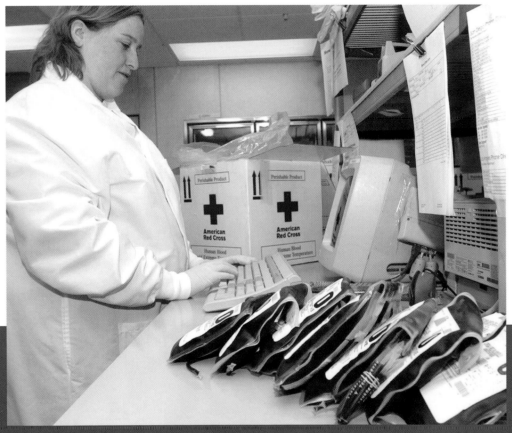

A member of the Red Cross handles blood donations made during the war in Iraq. The Red Cross continues to help people today—a testament to Barton's hard work and dedication.

medicines, food, and supplies for the rescue crews. The Red Cross raised and distributed a record $572.3 million to families of the victims, the businesses, and the residents devastated by the tragedy.

A LASTING LEGACY

From her childhood through her adult life, Barton kept a daily diary of her thoughts and feelings. In it, she described her personal experiences in great detail. She also wrote a steady stream of letters to her many friends and relatives. She told them fascinating stories of things she had

People today have been able to learn a lot about Barton from her diaries and letters. This is a letter that Barton sent to her secretary.

witnessed during wars, or in her travels. She candidly expressed her opinions on a wide variety of subjects. Hundreds of these letters have been saved. Because she was so famous, there were dozens of newspaper

A Symbol of Caring

For more than a hundred years, the Red Cross has been a symbol of caring and compassion. The identifying mark of a red cross on a white background was chosen to honor the society's Swiss founder, Jean Henri Dunant. It is simply a reversal of the Swiss flag, which is a white cross on a red background.

Many people think of the cross as a symbol of the Christian faith. However, the International Committee of the Red Cross is not associated with any particular religion. To avoid confusion in countries governed by leaders of other faiths, the Red Cross operates under different symbols there. In Muslim countries, the society is known as the Red Crescent. The Jewish chapter uses the Magen David Adom, or "Shield of David."

articles written about Barton during her lifetime. People who knew her often mentioned Barton in their own diaries and letters. For this reason, historians have a wealth of resources to draw from when studying Barton's life.

As a teacher, Clara Barton inspired in her students a love for learning. As a clerk, she brought order and efficiency to the U.S. Patent Office. Barton comforted thousands of dying men and rescued others from starvation and disease on the battlefields of the Civil War. In her service to the Red Cross, she helped needy people all over the world. Barton showed that women were capable of holding positions of leadership and responsibility. She did things no other woman had done simply because she refused to give up on her dreams. She always found a way to accomplish her goals.

When people think of Clara Barton today, they remember her as a woman of courage and compassion—a person who sacrificed her time, energy, and resources to help others. Her story will continue to inspire generations to come.

Timeline

CLARA BARTON'S LIFE   WORLD EVENTS

1821   Clarissa Harlowe Barton is born on December 25 in North Oxford, Massachussetts.

1839   Barton earns her teaching certificate and begins teaching elementary school.

1850   Barton attends the Clinton Liberal Institute in New York.

1852   Barton establishes New Jersey's first free public school.

1854   Barton accepts a position with the United States Patent Office in Washington, D.C.

1861   Barton nurses Union soldiers wounded in the first battles.

       The Civil War begins.

1862   Barton receives permission from the Surgeon General to nurse soldiers on the battlefield.

1863   The International Red Cross is founded in Geneva, Switzerland.

1865   The Civil War ends. Barton works to reunite prisoners of war with their families.

       The Civil War ends.

1869   Barton travels to Europe and learns about the work of the Red Cross.

1870 Barton serves with the International Red Cross in the Franco-Prussian War.

Franco-Prussian War begins.

1871 Franco-Prussian War ends.

1873 Barton returns to the United States and suffers a nervous breakdown, which keeps her confined to bed for two years.

1881 Barton establishes the American Red Cross Society and is elected its first president.

1882 The U.S. Senate ratifies the Treaty of Geneva, making it possible for the United States to join the International Committee of the Red Cross.

1884 Barton represents the United States at the Third International Conference of the Red Cross in Geneva, Switzerland.

1889 Barton directs the relief effort after the Johnstown Flood.

1896 Barton travels to Turkey to supervise relief to the victims of the Armenian massacres.

1898 Barton assists victims of the Spanish-American War and publishes *The Red Cross: A History*.

Spanish-American War begins in April. The fighting only lasts ten weeks.

1900 Barton spends six weeks serving victims of the Galveston Flood in Texas.

1904 Barton resigns from her position as president of the American Red Cross.

1907 Barton publishes her second book, *The Story of My Childhood*.

1912 Barton dies at home in Glen Echo, Maryland, on April 12 at the age of 90.

To Find Out More

BOOKS

Collins, David. *Clara Barton*. Uhrichsville, OH: Barbour & Co., 2000.

Herbert, Janis. *The Civil War for Kids.* Chicago: Chicago Review Press, 1999.

Marko, Eve. *Clara Barton and the American Red Cross.* New York: Playmore, Inc. 1995.

Quackenbush, Robert M. *Clara Barton and Her Victory Over Fear.* New York: Simon & Schuster, 1995.

Whitelaw, Nancy. *Clara Barton: Civil War Nurse.* Berkeley Heights, NJ: Enslow Publishers, 1997.

Woodworth, Deborah. *Compassion: The Story of Clara Barton.* Eden Prairie, MN: Child's World, 1997.

ORGANIZATIONS AND ONLINE SITES

The American Red Cross
http://www.redcross.org

This is the official site for the society. It includes information on the history of the organization, as well as current projects and opportunities for volunteers.

The Barton Center for Diabetes Education, Inc
http://www.clarabartoncamp.org

Named in honor of Clara Barton, this organization runs summer camps and special programs for children with diabetes, in Barton's hometown of North Oxford, Massachusetts. The site includes photos of Barton's family home and birthplace.

Clara Barton National Historic Site
http://www.nps.gov/clba

This site provides a virtual tour of Barton's home in Glen Echo, Maryland, which also served as the first headquarters of the American Red Cross and as a warehouse for disaster relief supplies.

Distinguished Women of Past and Present
http://www.distinguishedwomen.com/index.html

This lively site includes short biographies of famous women throughout history.

National Museum of Civil War Medicine
http://www.civilwarmed.org

Included on this site are numerous photos and detailed descriptions of museum exhibits on all aspects of medicine as it was practiced at the time of the Civil War.

A Note on Sources

Over the years, dozens of books have been written about Clara Barton. From her childhood through her adult life, Barton kept a daily diary of her thoughts and feelings. She also wrote a steady stream of letters to her many friends and relatives, telling them fascinating stories of things she had witnessed during the war or in her travels and candidly expressing her opinions on a variety of subjects. Hundreds of these letters have been saved. Because she was so famous, there were numerous newspaper articles written about Barton during her lifetime. People who knew her often mentioned Barton in their own diaries and letters. For this reason, historians have a wealth of resources to draw from when studying Barton's life.

Many children's books have been written about Barton, based primarily on her autobiography, *The Story of My Childhood*. However, in recent years, journalists have come to realize that Barton had a selective memory. What she wrote for publication was far different from what she wrote in her diary or in letters to close friends. She concealed things she thought might be disturbing to young readers or that would reflect badly on members of her family. She manipulated the dates and times of significant events in an effort to conceal her age. Thanks to Barton, many of these earlier biographies are inaccurate. Two exhaustive biographies of Barton have been written since the discovery of additional hidden diaries, and with increased access to relevant documents in the National Archives. *Clara Barton: Professional Angel* by Elizabeth Brown Pryor tells Barton's story in depth with warmth and honesty, describing not only her accomplishments but also her complex and compelling personality. In *Clara Barton: Woman of Valor*, Stephen Oats has written an equally thorough and detailed account that focuses on Barton's adventures during the Civil War and her experience as a woman of the nineteenth century.

—*Christin Ditchfield*

Index

About the Author

Christin Ditchfield is an author, conference speaker, and host of the nationally syndicated radio program *Take It To Heart!* She has interviewed celebrity athletes, such as gymnast Mary Lou Retton, NASCAR's Jeff Gordon, tennis pro Michael Chang, the NBA's David Robinson, and soccer great Michelle Akers. Her articles have been featured in magazines all over the world.

A former elementary-school teacher, Christin has written more than thirty books for children on a wide range of topics, including sports, science, and history. She recently wrote a biography of Condoleezza Rice for Franklin Watts. Ms. Ditchfield makes her home in Sarasota, Florida.